I Like Biographies!

Read About
Helen Keller

Stephen Feinstein

Enslow Publishers, Inc.

40 Industrial Road   PO Box 38
Box 398   Aldershot
Berkeley Heights, NJ 07922   Hants GU12 6BP
USA   UK

http://www.enslow.com

Words to Know

blind—Not able to see.

Braille—A special kind of writing for blind people.

deaf—Not able to hear.

water pump—A tool that helps bring water up from underground.

Presidential Medal of Freedom—An award that is given to Americans who do very good things for others.

Library of Congress Cataloging-in-Publication Data

Feinstein, Stephen.
    Read about Helen Keller / Stephen Feinstein.
        p. cm. — (I like biographies!)
    Includes bibliographical references and index.
    ISBN 0-7660-2299-4
    1. Keller, Helen, 1880–1968—Juvenile literature.
2. Blind-deaf women—United States—Biography—
Juvenile literature. I. Title. II. Series.
    HV1624.K4F45 2004
    362.4'1'092—dc21
    [B]
                                    2004000511

Printed in the United States of America

10 9 8 7 6 5 4 3 2 1

To Our Readers: We have done our best to make sure all Internet Addresses in this book were active and appropriate when we went to press. However, the author and the publisher have no control over and assume no liability for the material available on those Internet sites or on links to other Web sites. Any comments or suggestions can be sent by e-mail to comments@enslow.com or to the address on the back cover.

Illustration Credits: American Foundation for the Blind, Helen Keller Archives, p. 7; AP/Wide World, pp. 3, 17; Helen Keller Birthplace Foundation, Tuscumbia, Alabama, pp. 5, 9, 11, 15; Library of Congress, pp. 19, 22; Perkins School for the Blind, pp. 1, 13, 21.

Cover Illustration: Library of Congress.

Contents

Helen Keller 4

Helen Learns to Make Signs 6

Helen Learns That
Everything Has a Name 10

Helen Learns to Speak and Write . . 18

Timeline 22

Learn More 23

Index 24

Chapter 1

Helen Keller

Helen Keller was born on June 27, 1880. She was a bright and happy baby. When she was nineteen months old, Helen got very sick. A few days later her fever was gone, but something was wrong. Helen could not see anything. And she could not hear anything. Helen's mother and father were very sad.

These are Helen's parents, Kate and Arthur Keller.

Chapter 2

Helen Learns to Make Signs

Helen lived in a world she could not see. She had to feel things to learn what they were. Because she could not hear, Helen did not learn how to talk. She could not make people understand her. Often she got angry and would kick and scream. Helen cried a lot. She never laughed.

Helen could not see or hear. She was an unhappy child.

Helen needed to tell people what she wanted. So she used her hands. If Helen wanted something big, she spread her hands wide. If she wanted bread and butter, she would move her hands as if she were putting butter on bread. Helen made up hand signs for many things. But she still did not know any words.

Helen was born in this little house in Tuscumbia, Alabama. It is next to a big house where she lived with her family.

9

Chapter 3

Helen Learns That Everything Has a Name

When Helen was six, her parents found a teacher for her, Annie Sullivan. Annie gave Helen a doll. Then she slowly spelled out the letters "D-O-L-L" into Helen's hand. Helen moved her fingers the same way, spelling out "D-O-L-L."

Annie Sullivan came to live with the Kellers and help Helen learn. Annie and Helen were friends for many years.

11

Helen learned to spell many words
this way in the next few weeks. But she
did not understand what a word was.
She did not know that everything has
a name.

Annie helped Helen learn words by spelling
the letters out into Helen's hand. Then Helen
spelled them into Annie's hand.

One day, Helen and Annie were in the garden. When they came to the water pump, Annie pulled the handle up and down. Soon water flowed from the pump. Annie put Helen's hand into the water. At the same time, she spelled "W-A-T-E-R" into Helen's other hand.

This is the pump where Annie and Helen got water.

All of a sudden, Helen knew that "W-A-T-E-R" meant the cool stream flowing over her hand. All the shapes Annie made with her fingers had a meaning. Everything had a name!

The next words Helen learned were "H-E-L-E-N" and "T-E-A-C-H-E-R." Soon Helen learned the words for everything she touched.

Helen also learned words by putting her hands on a person's mouth while they were talking. She learned very quickly with Annie's help.

Chapter 4

Helen Learns to Speak and Write

In the next six months, Helen learned about six hundred words. Annie also taught Helen to read Braille, a kind of writing for the blind.

Helen learned to speak when she was ten. With Annie's help, Helen went to high school and college. While she was at college, Helen wrote *The Story of My Life*.

Helen worked very hard in college. She finished in 1904. She was twenty-four years old.

19

Helen became famous all over the world. She wrote more books. She gave speeches about the problems of the blind and the deaf. In 1964 she received the Presidential Medal of Freedom. Helen Keller died on June 1, 1968. She had spent her long life helping other people.

Helen became very famous because of her amazing life and all the help she gave to others.

21

1880—Helen is born in Tuscumbia, Alabama, on June 27.

1887—Annie Sullivan begins teaching Helen.

1903—Helen writes a book called *The Story of My Life*.

1904—Helen finishes college.

1964—Helen gets the Presidential Medal of Freedom.

1968—Helen dies on June 1.

Learn More

Books

Adler, David A. *Helen Keller*. New York: Holiday House, 2002.

Klingel, Cynthia, and Noyed, Robert B. *Helen Keller*. Chanhassen, Minn.: Child's World, 2002.

Larkin, Patricia. *Helen Keller and the Big Storm*. New York: Aladdin, 2002.

Internet Addresses

Helen Keller

<http://www.kidskonnect.com/HelenKeller/HelenKellerHome.html>

Helen Keller Kids Museum Online

<http://www.afb.org/braillebug/helen_keller_bio.asp>

Index

Braille, 18

Keller, Arthur (father), 4
Keller, Helen
   at college, 18
   childhood, 4, 6, 8,
     10, 12, 14, 16
   learning to speak, 18
   learning words, 16,
     18
   making speeches, 20
   using signs, 8
   writing books, 18, 20

Keller, Kate (mother), 4

Presidential Medal of
   Freedom, 20

Sullivan, Annie, 10, 12,
   14, 16, 18

The Story of My Life,
   18

water pump, 14